GW01459043

Raised Bed Vegetable Gardening-Complete: Growing Vegetables In Raised Bed Planters

By

James Paris

Published By

www.deanburnpublications.com

Blog: www.planterspost.com

1st Edition January 2016

ISBN-13: 978-1522970538

Relevant Books by Same Author

<u>Square Foot Gardening</u>

<u>Companion Planting</u>

<u>Straw Bale Gardening</u>

<u>Keyhole Gardening</u>

<u>HugelKultur Gardening</u>

<u>Lasagna Gardening</u>

Copyright

Table of Contents

INTRODUCING RAISED BED GARDENING

Growing vegetables in Raised Beds has become increasingly popular in recent years, for many good reasons be they environmental, financial, aesthetic, or just pure necessity!

The fact is however, no matter what your reasons for growing vegetables (or flowers) in Raised Beds, the results speak for themselves.

I am often asked "Is there anything I cannot plant in a Raised Bed Garden?" And my answer is always the same – "Anything that can be grown in a 'normal' garden can be grown better in a raised bed"

It may sound like a bold claim, but think about it – With this gardening technique you are simply enhancing the growing conditions of whatever you are growing, whilst at the same time removing anything that would normally restrict or even deny growth.

The fact is that in my opinion, growing vegetables in a raised bed is by far the easiest way of growing great vegetables without the huge labour involved when growing the traditional way.

Nothing however is without its cost, in both labour and financial expenditure, and it is true that to grow vegetables in a raised bed requires an element of both, especially at the early stages. This however need not put anyone off the idea, as the effort is minimal and short lived compared to the benefits derived from a raised bed garden that 'produces the goods'.

The raised bed gardener is able to spend longer tending to his plants than the average vegetable gardener, simply because he (or she) is not spending their valuable time digging over soil and clearing out weeds. For this reason alone the raised bed is preferable for those who are working all day and have limited time to spend in the evening tending their vegetable plot.

As you may have guessed by now, I am a firm believer in the advantages to be gained from growing fruit or vegetables in Raised Beds. In the next chapter You may find out why this is so...

Advantages of a Raised Bed Garden

As previously mentioned, I believe that Raised Beds have a number of advantages over the traditional 'row' style of gardening. Here are some examples that immediately spring to mind.

- **With a raised bed, it really does not matter what quality your garden soil is, or indeed what the drainage is like. As this is all added when forming your raised bed garden.**
- Easy to service/maintain. With a raised bed you have the advantage of height, which means that you do not have to bend over as far to take care of your vegetables. This is particularly advantageous if you are prone to suffer from back-ache.
- **Weed free. A raised bed is not troubled to nearly the same extent by the incursion of weeds, as all the soil/compost mix is freshly added. For any weeds that do appear, they are easier to remove as the compost mix does not compact like garden soil.**
- It is far easier to control destructive pests within a raised bed garden. This is simply because you are off the ground, and so keeping a natural barrier up in front of creeping pests like garden slugs.
- **With a slightly higher raised bed of around two feet, then you are not troubled quite as much with carrot fly for instance, who tend to be low fliers.**
- So out with back-breaking weeding tasks, along with digging over water logged soil and filtering out rocks and stones. In with easy gardening methods for the busy householder, and fresh vegetables for the whole family with the minimal of hassle.
- **Raised Beds are particularly suited to the physically disadvantaged and can be built to the ideal height to suit a user working from a wheelchair. Keeping a**

space of around 3 foot or 1 metre between beds also allows for easy access between multiple beds.

- A Raised Bed can be quickly 'converted' to form a simple polytunnel, or covered with butterfly mesh to stop the cabbage moth or birds from eating your crops. All kinds or arrangement can be constructed for growing climbing fruit or vegetable plants.
- **You can even build a raised bed garden on a hillside, making one side higher than the other, thus compensating for the slope and giving you a flat growing surface.**
- A raised bed does not get all compacted with people walking on, therefore no need to double-dig to loosen up the soil.

Building A Raised Bed Garden

A raised bed can be built with any one of a number of materials, the most popular being timber (treated or untreated). Other materials include, concrete, brick, corrugated sheet metal, sandbags, straw bales or concrete block work. In fact anything that you have to hand that can produce a decent barrier between 4 inched (100mm) and 2 foot (600mm) inches high, can be used to construct a Raised Bed garden.

Raised Bed Dimensions:

As to dimensions, this is really determined by many things including the space you have available, and indeed just exactly what your requirements are. Do you have a large family to feed, or do you intend to sell or barter (bartering is a great way to enjoy a diversity of produce from other gardeners) some of your produce ?

With all that considered, a typical raised bed vegetable plot is about 6 foot by 3 foot. This is an ideal size because it allows access from both sides, without you having to step onto the raised bed itself. This enables you to tend to your plants without treading on them in the process – always a good thing !

Another popular size is a simple square arrangement around 4 foot (1200mm) square to produce what has become known as a square foot garden. This simple technique can produce an amazing variety of vegetables throughout the growing season

As to depth. Overall you should aim for a minimum of 4 inches for a simple herb garden say, and up to 2 foot for root vegetables such as carrots and parsnips.
Bear in mind that the depth of the raised bed does not have to be the height of the sides, to explain a bit further. Say you would

like a bed depth of 18 inches (450mm), but you only have timber for 12 inch sides. Simply build your bed in the manner described in later chapters, and dig out the interior an extra six inches. This will enable you to fill in the bed with the compost of choice up to the required depth.

It should perhaps be pointed out here though, that this negates the concept of building a raised bed for the advantages to be gained with the height of the bed itself above ground, as will be explained later in the article. This system is mainly used where the existing soil is of poor quality and has to be replaced/substituted in order to grow the vegetables of your choice.

If you are building multiple raised beds, then they should be placed at least two feet (600mm) apart if possible – more if wheelchair access is required - to allow for easy access between them.

RAISED BED BEING BUILT WITH DECKING MATERIAL

Building a Timber Raised Bed

The construction of a timber raised bed is fairly simple and straight forward. First of all, level and mark out the area where you would like your raised bed to be. Bear in mind that it should not be under overhanging trees, and in an area where you can have easy access for tending your plants. It should get a minimum of 5-6 hours sunshine per day to produce best results for most vegetables.

For a 6 x 3 x 1.5 foot bed built using traditional decking timber, (I tend to use decking as it is stronger than just plain boards) you will need:

6 lengths decking @ 6' x 6" x 1"
6 lengths decking @ 2'10" x 6" x 1"
10 – 3" x 2" pointed posts @ 30"
Weed control fabric
Galvanized screws or nails
Wire mesh (optional)

Although the following instructions are aimed at an 'anchored' bed, it is also acceptable to simply make the corner posts the same depth as the bed itself, and lay the whole frame on the ground – the weight of soil will usually keep it anchored in place.

Begin by marking out with string and pegs, the area of your raised bed, putting down a peg on each corner. This is where you should consider whether or not you are going to dig out any of the existing ground.

Questions to ask yourself are, what depth of compost do I need, versus what height do I want the finished bed to be. If you are growing root vegetables that need depth, but you do not want the finished height to be over 1 foot for instance, then digging out the area to the depth required is your only option. This 'digging out' however may not be necessary if you have good quality topsoil. Simply loosen the existing soil with a garden fork and add your infill mix (more on this later) to the required level.

Once this decision is made, then we can proceed with building the raised bed. Once you have the pegs in the area that marks out the four corners of your raised bed, you simply take out one peg at a time and replace by hammering down your pointed posts, leaving them a minimum of 18 inches above the ground.

Alternatively, if you make these posts longer then you can use them as handy aids for lifting yourself up when tending your vegetables – just a matter of choice really.

The best way to do this is to put down one post at the end, then temporarily fix the first short end against the post. With this done, then hammer in the second post flush with the end of the 6" x 2" decking plank. Proceed with the two longer sides, then complete the other end. If you just put one screw partially home, then you can easily adjust to suit.

Be sure that you have leveled the timber and that you have left a minimum 12" in height above the first planks, so you are able to complete the job.

I find that it is better to construct with a cordless screwdriver as this does not impact the framework in the same way that hammer and nails does. Also should you make a slight error, then it is no trouble to take apart for adjustment.

Once this is done then simply mark out along the inside length two feet from each end, then making sure the construction is straight, hammer in two of the posts to the same height as the others. On the end of the construction, do the same with one post in the centre of the framework.

This will give you a strong sturdy construction, which you will need if you do not want the sides of your raised deck to bow under the pressure of the soil.

Point of note:

If you are building with heavier timbers, say 6" x 2" for instance then it may be possible to just put one post in the center of the long side and none at all on the end. I however tend to lean on the cautious side, and would rather aim for stronger option overall. Another tip is to put a cross brace in, if you are concerned about the sides bowing outward.

It is not an exact science, but there are minimum guidelines that must be kept to ensure a construction fit for purpose.

After you have built the sides then just screw down the remaining planking face down along the edge (as in the photograph), to make a comfortable sitting or leaning area for tending to your raised bed.

One thing to consider during this time, is whether or not you are bothered by Gophers or Moles. If you are, then at this point you would place in 1" galvanized wire mesh, covering the bottom of your raised bed. This will be extremely effective in stopping the varmints from destroying your crop and giving you endless grief and heartache!

The weed control fabric should be fixed down the inside of the bed, to keep the wet soil away from the timber. This will help the timber to breathe and make it just that bit longer lasting.

2nd Point of note: Do not use timber that has been treated with creosote, as this may weep through and kill the plants!

If you think you may wish to move them to another location perhaps in the next season, then it is probably best not to hammer the corner posts into the ground and instead make them the actual height of the bed itself.

In other words your 18 inch high bed will just need 18 inch high posts instead of 30 inches or so. These will be fixed in the same way to the corner posts and the infill will hold the whole construction in place – though not as well as the former method!

Here is an example of a larger construction 9 foot in length and 18 inches high. As you can see, this bed is built to sit upon a concrete base. Built with three rows of decking, it has 2 centre braces made from 3 x 2 to keep it solid.

Possibly the simplest form of Raised Bed is the 4 foot square model. This can be constructed from decking material by simply adding a short corner post at each corner and fixing it together with decking screws. Everything else is constructed the same way as the larger deck.

Materials needed would be ..

2 lengths decking @ 4' x 6" x 1"
2 lengths decking @ 3'10" x 6" x 1"
4 – 2" x 2" pointed posts @ 18"
Weed control fabric
Galvanized screws or nails
Wire mesh (optional)

Again, you have the option to simply use 6 inch posts at the corners if you have no need to 'lock in' to the ground area.
To create a 'Square Foot Garden then simply add a 'grid' as in the picture below using garden canes or even twine to mark out the foot-square areas for planting.

Regarding Timber: Some people have concerns over whether or not to use treated or untreated timber to build their Raised Beds. This is perfectly understandable as more of us become aware of the possibility of contamination regarding chemicals that have been used to treat the timbers.

There are 2 main issues to consider here, and that is the effect that treated timber may have on the plants themselves. And the effect that may be had to the consumer of these same vegetables – if indeed they survive!

Modern timber treatment via tanalisation methods according to the soil association (www.soilassociation.org) is perfectly suitable for gardening structures such as Raised Beds or compost bins – provided the timber has been purchased already treated.

Various blogs will insist that there could be an issue with the chemicals leeching out of the timber, but I have found no evidence for this – although I do agree that it is unwise to use treated timber sawdust in the compost for instance, and that I would not use it on the barbeque where toxins could be released into the atmosphere – and your food!

'Old' methods such as the creosote that would be used on timber railway sleepers however is definitely hazardous to the plants themselves, and should be avoided for any planting constructions – unless it is covered or lined with a suitable polythene membrane. In fact I recommend lining timber Raised Beds anyway as this reduces water leakage and lengthens the life of the timbers.

If the plants foliage comes into contact with creosote then it will wither and die, simple as that.

To sum-up. As far as I can deduct there is no real evidence to show that plants grown in treated timber structures, do in any way absorb the chemicals that have been used to treat the timber.

That being said however – If in doubt simply use untreated timber or line with polythene membrane. Even an untreated timber bed will still give you at least 5-7 years of use before it starts to decay.

Building a raised bed from brick

If you are fully convinced that the position of your raised bed is permanent or that you will never need to move it to somewhere else; then the option of building a solid brick construction is open to you.

The advantages of a brick-built raised bed are simply that it will not rot, and is a sound structure not easily damaged. Disadvantages are that of course, you cannot move it to another position without destroying it, and also it can look quite unsightly depending on the surroundings. If for instance you have a brick-walled garden, then it may blend in very nicely.

Materials that you will need for your brick-built raised bed are as follows, based on a 6 x 3 construction:

Approximately 400 common brick
Sand and cement
Crushed gravel
Concrete ballast

With any brick construction then you have to build a foundation, otherwise the construction will crack as it subsides into the ground. This is quite a simple construction overall, but you may feel more comfortable getting a builder to do it if you have no experience at this sort of thing. However if you are at all interested, I would suggest that it is a good time to try out your building skills!

Begin by marking out and leveling the ground, as in the preceding chapter. When this is done, then dig out a trench for your foundation, bearing in mind that the brickwork has to be roughly centre of the foundation. The trench should be about 12 inches deep (for frost cover) and 12-18 inches wide, if you are building with 4" brick. This allows for a good concrete raft to build upon. If you are building in an area not bothered by penetrating frost then this trench can be shallower – or deeper if you have the opposite problem.

Mix up a concrete mix with your concrete ballast using a 5 – 1 mixture. That is 5 parts ballast to 1 part concrete. Add water and mix thoroughly. Fill the bottom of the trench a minimum of 3 inches deep with this concrete mix. This will ensure a good solid foundation for your construction.
In just a couple of days this will be dry enough to proceed with the building process.

Top Tip:
If you want to shortcut this process a little, then for this construction it is possible to simply lay 4" concrete block on a bed of cement mix, to form a ready-made foundation for your walls.

Once the foundation has been laid then it is time to put your building skills to the test. Main thing here if you have no experience with building is to string a line along the edge of your construction, and follow it. **Keep the spirit level at work** and be sure not to deviate from the line.

Mix up your sand and cement to a 3 to 1 mix. Three parts sand to one part cement. Add a plasticizer to the water before using as this will make things a lot easier when it comes to spreading the compo. Cement mix should be about ½ inch deep and the same at the ends. Each brick must be laid level, with a slight tap to bed-in. Be sure to overlap each brick as you are building, and tie in at the corners.

On the first layer to rise above the ground level, you should include a few 'weep holes'. This is simply done by keeping a couple of bricks without compo at the joints and leaving a gap instead.

Once you have reached the full height, you can either just finish off with a bed of cement over the top bricks, smoothing to form a half curve. Or you can finish with a concrete coping from the builders suppliers.

In the right situation however you can even build the structure without the use of mortar at all. This can be especially handy if you are looking for a temporary structure that can be moved or dismantled at the end of the season – perhaps to be moved to another area the following year.

The simple potato planter below is built with a mixture of old bricks and concrete blocks, that have been laid without any mortar. The strength simply comes from the overlapping of the brickwork. This is sufficient in strength to hold in the growing mix throughout the season.

Concrete Block Raised Bed

Similar to the earlier construction, this is made from concrete block, laid flat; this is a simple construction that can be taken down when and if, it's not needed any longer. Owing to the pure weight of the block however, it is far stronger than the dry-laid brick model.

If you use 18" x 9" x 4" dense block, then layout a flat area for the base, pounding in some crushed rock for a foundation. After making sure your foundation track is perfectly level, using a straight edge; Start to lay your block on the flat side down on a bed of rough sand.

This row must be perfectly level otherwise you will face problems as the structure rises. Make sure that you overlap the blocks so that there is no break going up through the wall.

The down side with this raised bed is that you will use twice the concrete block as building normally, however you will save on sand and cement as well as time.

Drywall Example Above

Finished result should be a solid construction that has a good broad top to sit on while working your raised bed. True, it takes up a bit more space, but overall it is perhaps the simplest and quickest way to build. Just be sure of the first layer, and everything else will follow on.
Be sure that you tie in the corners using the same building method, overlapping the blocks at the corners as well as the sides.

Top Tip: If you would like a more secure finish, then simply lay the top row of block on a bed of cement mortar. This will secure the whole structure quite nicely

Other Raised Bed Examples

There is actually no limit to the amount of ways to construct a raised bed garden area, or indeed the different materials that can be used for it. Or perhaps I should say that the only real limit is your imagination!

Corrugated iron sheeting, properly supported is often used to create a raised bed. It has to be said though that if you are building for appearance, then this is probably not the one for you !

Timber logs cut straight from the tree. These can look especially effective and can be built similar to a log cabin construction, giving an extremely strong and versatile structure that will last for many years.

Old Railway sleepers. I would not particularly recommend using old railway sleepers, as there is a danger of creosote leaking into your plant bed, causing a health hazard – as well as killing the plants. If old sleepers are used then be sure to line the inside with polythene barrier to prevent this happening.

In general however the **modern railway sleepers** for sale in your local garden centre will not have been treated with creosote, but with a plant-friendly injection treatment. This makes them ideal for raised bed construction. Rot – resistant cedar or redwood are the best railway ties for building your raised bed. Consult the sales person before purchasing.

Build using the same principles above for the timber raised bed, but because of the heavy timber (about 19" x 5") you need only use support at the corners, except for the really long lengths at over 3 meters.

Filled sandbags. Yes even sandbags can easily be utilized to form a Raised Bed of virtually any size. Simply fill and layer the bags as you would when building a brick wall. This is a quick and simple method to create an effective planting area.

Straw Bale Bed

Straw Bales can also be used to form a Raised Bed Garden, and they have the added advantage in that they can be used to plant in as well. In effect your 'wall' becomes a planting area as well as the internal space being created.

Start by sitting the bales on edge (pointy ends downward) and creating a suitably sized area. This should be no wider than arms reach to the center of the area. Once set in place then tie a length of strong string around the whole area to hold the bales in place, before infilling the space created in the middle.

Alternatively use canes or wooden stakes to hold the bales in place.

Growing vegetables in straw bales or Straw Bale Gardening, is a whole new area and needs a more dedicated platform than this book. However here are the basics behind Straw Bale Gardening and how you would go about preparing your bales for planting – yes they do need prepared before anything will even attempt to grow in them!

Setting up/Feeding:

When placing the bale itself, it is important that it is arranged cut side up, or on edge. This enables the water to seep right to the inside of the bale and begin the 'cooking' process.

If you inspect the bales you will notice that one of the two cut sides consists of folded straw and the other is clean-cut straw? This clean-cut side is the one that faces upward.

This allows the water and fertilizer to run down to the inside of the bale and remain trapped. It is not a complete disaster if you get this wrong, but the bale will tend to dry out quicker as it will not hold the water as efficiently.

The 2 strings that hold the bale in place should be running along the sides. It is important that you leave these strings in place – for obvious reasons!

This 'cooking' is where the bale begins the process of decomposing and thereby producing heat in the inside of the bale, which in turn breaks down the straw and prepares it for your plants to benefit.

Once you have the bale in place then you must feed and water it to begin the process. Feeding is very important as the straw bale itself is mainly just carbon (hay differs as per the previous chapters) , and your vegetables will need a good mixture of nitrogen and potash to develop fully.

This feeding can be achieved in several ways. Either through conventional fertilizers or store-bought organic fertilizer or, home-brewed organic feeds.

In my experience I have found that organic fertilizers do not have enough nitrogen content to 'kick-start' the cooking-off period. For this reason I would recommend a good nitrogen-rich lawn fertilizer for this period, and then feed organically over the growing season as necessary.

Do not choose the 'slow release' fertilizers available. Instead go for the cheaper (and more effective for our purpose) soluble lawn fertilizer.

The **store bought nitrogen-rich feeds** should be spread over the bale at the beginning and watered in. Thereafter added to the water itself is often best before the bale is soaked.

Organic home-brew is simple to make and apply. Preparation should be done a few days before you are ready for the bale.

Add a few good handfuls of grass, stinging nettles, or borage which has been cut into pieces, to a pail of water. Weigh it down with a heavy stone or brick, then leave for 7 days to infuse.

The resulting liquid can be diluted at roughly 1 part feed to 10 parts water, then applied to the bale. The remaining liquid can be topped-up over the season with more plant material and water, and applied as necessary.

Compost feed can be produced by taking a few handfuls of compost and adding to water and left to infuse as previously described.

Manure feed is especially rich in nitrogen which your veggies will love, however it is the 'stinky' option! To make this tea place a shovel of manure (horse, sheep, rabbit chicken, or goat is ideal) into a hessian sack and put inside a deep pail of water for 5-7 days.

Squish the sack up and down a bit before removing from the pail (you can add it to the compost heap). The resulting tea should be watered down about 15 parts water to 1 part tea.

Be aware however that using fresh manure does carry an element of risk with regard to E.coli and other harmful bacteria and worm larvae that may be present.

With that in mind do take precautions when handling fresh manure, or alternatively (and safer) use well composted manure that has been composting for at least 1 year.

Also, do not use manure compost on any low-ground vegetables that may come into direct contact with it such as cucumber or courgette for instance.

Fish meal, bone meal and seaweed also are great sources of nitrogen, potassium and other nutrients that will benefit your vegetables.

Priming The Bale:

The actual process of priming your bale should be done in the following sequence..

Day 1: Soak the bale completely with water infused with nutrients, or prepare the bale by scattering some store-bought fertilizer over it before soaking.

Day's 2-5: Continue with the soaking and feeding process. Monitor the internal temperature with a thermometer (a compost or meat temperature probe is ideal), and watch for the rise in temperature as the 'cooking' process begins.

Day's 6-14: Water every alternate day, checking to see that the bale does not dry out. As the process of cooking out comes to an end, the bale will cool down to reflect a temperature just a little higher or equivalent to, the ambient external temperature.

This means that the bale is ready to plant. If the reading is still high then wait till it drops before attempting to plant, otherwise it will be too hot for the roots and the plant will likely suffer a premature death!

Planting Out The Bale

Now that you bale has 'cooked out' ** and the composting process has begun, you are ready to plant the vegetables of your choice.

There will be more details regarding the individual vegetables and their growing needs in later chapters, for now however we shall look at the steps to be taken in order to get the best out of your bale.

** This 'cooking' process is not always evident, especially if you live in a damp, cold climate. If this is the case and you do not see very much evidence of a temperature rise within the bale, do not despair! In some cases I have known the bales to show no (or little) sign of heating up in this fashion, but as the season goes forward and the temperatures rise the bale will indeed compost down and produce good results.

My advice is to give it a good 3 weeks during which you are following the feeding regime, then to carry on with your planting. If by some chance the bale does indeed suddenly start producing heat you may well find that you will have to replant once it has cooled down, but in my own experience this has never proved to be the case.

Plants or Seeds?

The first decision is whether you intend to plant young developed plants, or plant direct from seed. Either way is possible for your straw bale garden, but the process differs as per the instructions below.

Planting from seed is possible by covering the flat surface of the bale about 2 inches deep in a good potting compost. This should reach to about 2 inches from the edge of the bale itself.

Once this is done then simply poke a hole with your finger at the spacing's needed for your seeds, and place the seed in the holes.

For small seeds such as onions, then sow sparingly in rows as you would in a conventional garden.

Planting young seedlings is a simple matter of chopping into the bale and digging out a suitable area (usually 4-6 inches deep and 3-4 inches across) and after removing your plant from its pot, placing it in the hole.

Firm around with more good potting compost before watering thoroughly.

Feeding: Although the bale should by now be thoroughly infused with nutrients thanks to your feeding efforts, your plants will need further feeding especially when they begin to produce fruits or otherwise mature.

Once per week with your organic tea should be adequate for most vegetables. With a heavy crop of fruiting tomatoes however, I would increase the dosage to twice per week.

For complete instructions and information on building your own Straw Bale Garden then please check out the link at the beginning of this book.

Square Foot Bed

Another interesting idea for a raised bed garden is to follow the principle of the 'square foot' gardening method. Square foot gardening is simply taking a structure of four foot by four foot, and separating them into one foot squares by

means of a simple framework placed over the top of the area. This can be done with canes as in the above example, strips of timber, or taught nylon string.

This gives sixteen potential 'mini plots' to work with. The idea here is that a family of four can actually produce enough vegetables throughout the growing season to feed them all comfortably and cheaply.

Unbelievable as this may sound, it is indeed possible if enough thought has gone into the preparation and a good rotational plan is followed. One of the good things about this plan (and there are many) is that the plot should never need to be artificially fertilized as the vegetables in each plot take only the nutrients that they need, and as they move around they leave the other nutrients for the plants that come along behind.

As an example of this, you have grown beans and peas. They take nitrogen from the air, and leave it in the soil. Thus it is good to let these plants die at the end of their growing season and in turn fertilize the soil with a nitrogen rich environment for vegetables such as Cabbage Cauliflower or kale that love this environment.

As in fact do potatoes, though they should not be planted alongside brassicas as they prefer different pH levels.
This is in fact the traditional crop rotation method in miniature and works very well for the four foot square garden.

If we simply take this method and place it into a six by four foot raised bed, then you would have twenty four potential planting areas. This is more than enough for the average family needs of vegetables, if it is properly handled.

Hot Bed Raised Bed

An extremely effective way to get an early start with your RBG is to use it as a 'Hot' Bed. There are 2 main ways to effectively create a hot bed – artificial, with the help of hot water or electricity. Or natural, with the help of decomposing organic material.

Using either of these techniques means a longer growing season as you can start earlier and finish later owing to the warmer nature of the growing medium.

An artificial Hot Bed can be created by laying a special layer of electric cable or blanket about 6-12 inches (150-300mm) below the surface. This depth is largely determined by the root depth of the plant you are growing.

Most soil heating cables are thermostatically set at around 70F (21c) although the more expensive models have adjustable thermostats fitted.

Make sure you have an electricity outlet close by. Lay out the cable according to the manufacturer's instructions, then cover over with soil – job done!

The electric soil heater technique has the advantage of being quick to fit, and manageable with regard to heat control. However on the downside is the cost of the electricity – or indeed the supply itself.

An organic Hot Bed is a little more 'manual' but has the advantage in that it does not run up your electric bill, and feeds the crops over a long period – meaning no need for artificial fertilizers.

These organic beds are usually created within a cold-frame or Raised Bed. Either way in order to work effectively they have to be covered over to preserve the heat generated.

This heat is generated by a layer of fresh manure, preferably horse manure. I emphasize the word 'fresh' If the manure has already decomposed then there will be little or no heat generated, and all you will have is the nutrient benefits of the manure itself.

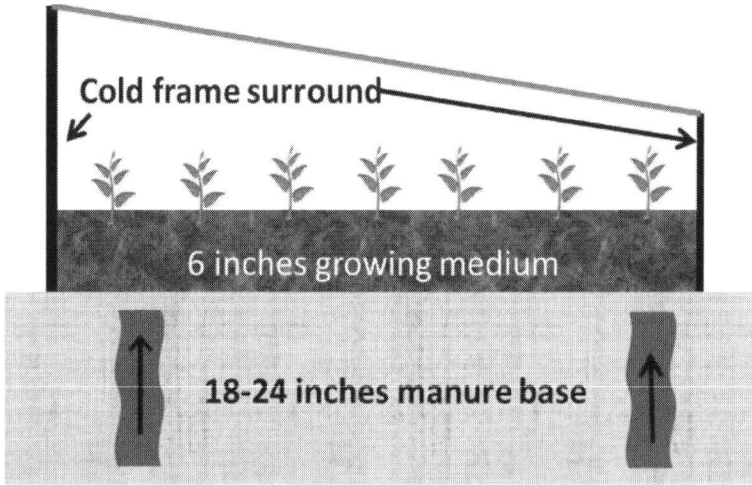

As you may see from the illustration above. Fresh manure is placed in a trench, and the growing medium layered on top. As the manure begins to decompose it heats up the bed.

The details are simple no matter how you achieve the end goal. After placing the manure in the trench – or the complete base of the frame as in the preceding illustration – trample it down firmly, and soak completely before covering over with soil.

This will 'kick-start' the decomposition process, and assure you of good results. A compost thermometer is handy in this instance to keep a check on the ground temperature before planting, otherwise especially in the early stages it may get too hot for the young plants.

The heating aspect of a hot bed of this nature does not last forever – maybe 3-4 months. However the nutrients produced by the manure will last for many months – even into the next season.

If you have a greenhouse or polytunnel, then a Hot Bed can be very effective over the winter months for keeping the inside temperatures just above freezing. This makes it an effective way to over-winter plants that cannot withstand severe frosts.

The way to achieve this is simply to make a wooden frame and pack in the fresh manure as before, covering lightly with soil. Leave uncovered. This will act as a warm radiator for your polytunnel.

MY NOTES / TO-DO PAGE

Filling and Modifications

Filling the raised bed:

Next we come to filling your raised bed. This starts with the drainage at the base. This can be broken pots or rough broken brickwork, built to about three inches deep. However before this you may want to consider whether or not you are bothered by moles, gophers, voles etc.

These creatures are likely to follow the worms or fresh shoots up into your raised bed if you allow it to happen.

If you are in any doubt then lay out your 1" galvanized wire mesh at the base of the bed, before putting in your drainage level – better safe than sorry ! Also a layer of tough weed suppressant material at this stage, laid over the mesh will help keep out the burrowers

Once you have laid out your mesh, then put in the layer of drainage as described above. If you have a well-drained soil around you, or under the bed then this can naturally be adapted to suit.

The drainage should then be layered over with a minimum of 3-4 inches of soil mixed with compost.

Composting:

In a nutshell, compost is the term used for organic matter that has been decomposed (rotted) and recycled as a soil conditioner, to improve crop growth performance.

This is something that you must think about long before you need the compost, in most cases a year at least. Your SFG needs compost that is well rotted and crumbly to the feel. If it is still smelly then it is not ready for the garden yet.

The process of making your own compost is simple enough, as it is basically a load of organic material such as vegetable trimmings, grass cuttings, fallen leaves etc, that are dumped into a bin or wooden framework and left to decompose in a process that can take months or even years. That's the simple answer; however there are certain things that you **should not add** to a compost heap such as..

- **Inorganic material:** Plastic and polythene will not break down to form compost. Obvious I know, but it had to be said!
- **Pet Poop:** Never add dog or cat droppings to the compost heap, as this can add several disease organisms that can turn your compost toxic.
- **Fish, fats, meat, bones and dairy**: These should not be added as they can just attract vermin, and cause your compost to smell badly.
- **Coal ash**: timber ash is fine for compost as it adds valuable potash, but coal ash is not as it can add high levels of sulphur to your compost.
- **Coloured paper**: Coloured paper can contain heavy metals and other toxic materials. These should not be added to your compost.
- **Diseased plants**: Any diseased or infested plants that you have to lift up should be burned or otherwise disposed of. Do not add to the compost as they will most likely end up back in your garden to repeat the cycle all over again!

Compost Mixes:

There are many different mixes of compost that will suit certain plants more than others, and this is great if you are specializing in a specific area like growing giant pumpkins! However if you have a source of well-rotted manure, then this is ideal for crops such as tomatoes, beans, peas, leeks - in fact just about anything, as rotted manure is a great source of nitrogen which every plant needs in different quantities.

There are certain plants that also make valuable additions to the compost heap such as nettles, which speed up decomposition and add valuable nitrogen, or comfrey, which is a terrific source of potash (potassium) and has a high carbon to nitrogen ratio – which is ideal for most plants and perfect for tomatoes, fruit and berries.

If you are working a homestead or hobby farm then you almost certainly have access to chicken manure! This is very rich in nitrogen and a fantastic addition to your compost. Be sure though to let it rot for at least 1 year to kill off any parasites or eggs that may be in it; also it needs this time to 'mellow' otherwise it is too strong in nitrogen for most plants to tolerate.

When using manure of any kind you have the option to add it to your composting heap while they are both still in the process of decomposing; or you may add the fully decomposed manure directly to your SFG as part of the mix.

When has manure decomposed enough to use?
You will know when the manure has finished decomposing when it has a deep 'earthy' smell – not smelling of dung; and the

material itself should be relatively dry and crumbly when handled.

If it still smells of dung then it has not finished decomposing and should be left for a further few weeks or even months.

Here is a chart to show just what the different animal dungs 'bring to the table' with regard to percentage values of nutrients.

	NITROGEN	PHOSPHORUS	POTASH
Average farmyard manure	0.64	0.23	0.32
Pure pig dung	0.48	0.58	0.36
Pure cow dung	0.44	0.29	0.49
Horse Manure	0.49	0.29	0.58
Deep litter on straw	0.80	0.55	0.48
Fresh Poultry Dung	1.66	0.91	0.45
Pigeon Dung	5.84	2.10	1.77

As you may notice from this chart – it would pay to keep in with your local pigeon fancier – or keep some birds yourself!

The compost itself, will largely depend on what you are about to grow. For instance, if you are growing carrots or parsnips, then a light loamy compost with a good mix of sand may be required. Potatoes or leeks may require a good bed of well-rotted manure layered over the soil at the base.

It should be pointed out that the internal filling of any raised bed should not be soil alone, as this has a tendency to go rather solid after a short time. Instead mix some quality topsoil together with a good loamy compost, with plenty of organic material to keep it well drained and nutrient-rich. Again depending on your choice of vegetable a slow release fertilizer or well-rotted manure could be mixed through.

Here are some examples of infill mixes I use in my Raised Beds – and produce some excellent results!

Mix 1: 50% compost, 20% washed sand, 30% peat moss.

Mix 2: 40% compost, 20% fish meal, 30% coconut coir and 10% good topsoil.

Mix 3: 50% compost, 20% vermiculite (or perlite), 30% peat moss.

Mix 4: 50% compost, 30% peat moss, 20% quality topsoil.

Mix 5: 40% compost, 40% peat moss, 20% vermiculite.

Hard work?
Ok, to be fair you may well be thinking that this sounds like a lot of hard graft – for something that is supposed to be an easy gardening method ? Well yes you could be right…However, once this part is done then you can relax and actually enjoy the next part, which is planting your vegetables. From now on it's easy street !

At this stage, and throughout the growing season you will discover just why raised bed gardening is so much easier than the traditional vegetable garden. Look over at your neighbour breaking his back hoeing between the vegetables, or digging his way through stony ground. Whilst all the time you are sitting on the side of your raised bed easily pulling out a few weeds, and plucking your ripe tomatoes.

Modification1 – Cold frame

One of the simplest and yet most rewarding conversions you can make to your raised bed garden, is to turn it into a cold-frame. This will enable you to get an early start in the growing season with all your early plants such as tomatoes.

If you stay in colder northern climes, then this can become an almost permanent answer to a greenhouse, enabling you to grow things like cucumbers, marrows, chillies and tomato plants – to name just a few.

To do this is quite simple and will any take a short time. Start before you infill the raised bed with any compost material as it will be much simpler. Material needed for the job:

1 ½ " plastic pipe
Galvanized pipe straps
½" flexible pvc tubing or similar
Polythene sheeting

Cut out eight lengths of 1 ½" plastic pipe, the kind used for domestic plumbing is just fine, measure so that they do not protrude above the wall of the bed when placed vertically inside. Next space evenly along the inside wall of the bed, pointing upward, and secure in place using galvanized pipe straps, top and bottom.
When this is done then cut the ½ " tubing to about twice the width of the raised bed. Bend the pipe and slip into place.

To stop the bent tubing slipping all the way down the pipe, simply fill with some fine gravel or even a sand and cement mix up to about 4" (100mm) from the top of the pipe. Once this is done you will have an effect similar to the covered wagons you see in the old western movies !

Next you simply fit the polythene over the framework. This is easiest done by securing the polythene sheet along one side of the frame by a length of 2 x 1 for instance. Then you simply pull over the frame when you want it covered.
The ends are a bit more awkward, but if you leave plenty material to work with, then you can simply weigh down by placing a plank on top of the polythene, and weigh down with bricks or equivalent.

The following picture below shows a smaller version of that described, but using just a part of the raised bed area.

One thing you may note is that this model can be improved by the addition of slits or vent holes in the polythene. Better still fit it with polythene that has holes in it especially for the purpose, as in the example above where only part of the raised bed is used for bringing on the seedlings.

This style of perforated polythene will prevent your 'polytunnel' from overheating.
Failing that then you must remember to remove or fold back the sheeting when appropriate. This is especially true if your intention is just to use it for the hardening of young plants.

Modification 2 – Insect/Bird netting

Another good thing about the raised bed is just how easy it can be covered up to stop the predations of birds or insects. The simplest way to do this is to follow the previous example for creating the frame effect, but replacing the polythene with a fine bird mesh.

This can be easily clipped into place in a few minutes, keeping your plants free from not only birds such as wood pigeons, blackbirds etc; but also stopping the cabbage butterfly for instance, from laying it's eggs on your plant leaves.

Another way however to do this is to follow the example in the picture. This is simple loops made from plumbers pipe and nailed to the frame.

This in turn gives you a structure that you are able to walk around in, whilst tending your vegetables.

It would only take a simple modification to convert this into a temporary polytunnel, if you used polythene instead of nylon mesh.

Yet another way to cover up, is to raise up a post on each corner of the raised bed, link together with a 2 x 2 along the top, between the four corners.
This will give you an effect like a four poster bed, which you can then cover with your material of choice.

As you can see, there are several ways to cover your raised bed, either to use as a cold-frame or to simply protect against birds and insects. All these ways will only take a very short time, and will reap great rewards.

Modification 3 – Automatic Irrigation

Another addition to your raised bed can be an irrigation system. This can be an automatic irrigation system, or it can simply be a system that is put in place, and watered when you choose to do so. There are many watering systems on the market, but here is a simple model to follow that will do the job fine.

Place ½" polythene pipe under the soil just an inch or so, shaped like a tuning fork, with the single end at the top attached to a fitting such as a 'hoselock' click fit type. This can simply and easily be put together with 2 push fit elbows and 1 tee piece. 2 end caps close of the end of the pipes
The pipe should be perforated along its length with small drip emitters fitted every 12 inches.

After fitting a stop valve at the raised bed end, the whole system should them be fitted to a water tank - the bottom of the tank raised above the top level of the bed.

This tank can be attached to the mains water supply if needed, or it can be filled manually. with a float valve to close it of when the supply is not needed.

By turning the water valves on, the drip emitters will release a small amount of water over any given period. After some 'fine tuning' this is a system that will take away a lot of the labour attached to watering a vegetable garden.

Working Tips For A Raised Bed

When it comes to tending a raised bed garden, there are a few differences, or subtleties compared to tending a traditional vegetable patch.

Here are a few tips for making life even easier !

Cut a strong 'spanner board' i.e. a board that is slightly longer than the width of your bed. Place across the bed, resting on each side edge. This can be used for placing your small garden tools on when working the bed, without leaving them in the wet soil. A good place also to put a glass of something cool !

Avoid standing in the raised bed. This is to prevent the soil becoming compacted, and also to prevent any chance that you will push out the sides of the raised bed, by compressing the soil over time.

If you have multiple raised beds, then put down a weed restricting fabric between them and cover with 2-3 inches of mulching material such as chipped bark. This saves a lot of laborious weeding between the beds, and leaves more time for what really matters in life.

Plants can be grown a little closer together in a raised bed, because of the concentrated nature of the feeding system.

Another good tip and one that will keep the slugs and snails at bay, is to place a copper slug tape or strip around the timber structure. Slugs hate copper because of the way it reacts to the slug mucus, so they will not cross it. If you have no copper tape and have an immediate slug problem, try spraying a concentrated salt solution around the outside base

of the bed. This can be quite effective, but do not let any into your plant bed as it will most likely kill your vegetables !

Working a raised bed garden as can be seen here is slightly different for the 'normal' way of gardening – but not so different that you need a new set of rule books so to speak. When speaking to raised bed gardeners, you will probably find that the biggest difference is the fact that they are not suffering from constant backache!

The raised bed is much easier when it comes to weed control – mainly because you have started by using virgin soil that is weed free to begin with. However even after it has been up a while, it is still much easier to weed owing to the softer loamier make-up of the soil or compost.

Even the feeding of the plants is more successful, as all the nutrients are going to the plants and not seeping away into the soil, as is normally the case.

Building multiple raised beds, if you have the space, is ideal. This allows for a good rotation of the different crops and guarantees a great harvest year after year.

VEGETABLES FOR A RAISED BED

What vegetables would I recommend to grow in a raised bed ? Just about anything !

Seriously, there is nothing I can think of that will not grow as well if not better in a raised bed, than it would in a traditional vegetable plot. The mere fact that the vegetables are raised up away from the creeping things of the soil, means that they have better protection against insects, and are not so prone to fungal disease as they have better air circulation in general.

For instance, cucumbers will grow better as they can be trailed over the edge of the bed, keeping them of the ground. Or indeed they can be grown over a simple frame-work fixed to the side of the Raised Bed.
Carrots are a crop where it is better to grow them in a Raised Bed anyway, in order to help protect from the carrot fly. Potatoes can be easier to dig up from a raised bed, as can parsnips and any deep rooted vegetables, simply because the soil is looser – meaning that you are far less likely to get the 'forked' look of carrots grown in stony soil.

It is much easier on the back when tending strawberries or any low growing fruit or vegetable. However, tomatoes grow exceedingly well in raised bed situations, as they can greatly benefit from a concentrated feeding regime of the type a raised vegetable garden offers.

It is a simple matter to build any kind of trellis work on a Raised Bed – particularly the timber models, as it is easier to secure any fixings into. Growing beans or peas in a raised bed complete with trellis or framework is a simple matter when working a raised bed vegetable garden.

Here are some further examples as a guide to planting out a
Raised Bed Garden

Planting Out Your Raised Bed

What to plant

When deciding what to plant in your raised bed, there are a
number of things to take into consideration. These could include
the following:

**How many raised beds do you have to plant? More than one
bed means that you can have a larger crop of one single
vegetable kind.**

How big is your family, or how many do you intend to feed?

**Does your raised bed get full sun, i.e. at least 6-8 hours per
day?**

What do you like to eat? This may sound like a silly question;
however it is easy to grow something just because you can. Only
to find that it is wasted at the end of the season because you do
not really like Brussel sprouts for instance!

**Did you use this bed last year, and if you did, what did you
grow on it? Good crop rotation is key to getting a great
harvest.**

As you may understand, what to plant is a question that has many
answers depending on your individual wants and needs – as well
as the wants and needs of your friends and neighbors!
For this reason I will cover a few different planting regimes that
hopefully may give you some ideas of your own.

Crop types

First of all we must divide the crops into their respective families, in order to get the best out of the soil conditions they are planted in.

Root Crops: Potatoes, carrots, parsnips, beetroot, fennel, celery

Brassicas: Cabbage, Brussel sprouts, cauliflower, broccoli, radish, swede turnip

Legumes: Peas, mange tout, French and broad beans

Alliums (onion family): Shallots, onions, garlic, chives, leeks

Solanaceae: Aubergine, potato, tomato, peppers, eggplant

Cucurbits: Cucumber, squash, pumpkin, melon, marrow

Miscellaneous: All fruits, lettuce, herbs, sweetcorn, chicory, asparagus

Though this is by no means an extensive list, it does give a good selection of the most commonly grown vegetables, and is more than enough to get started with!

Watch your height
One of the things that is easy to over-look, but most important, is to be aware of the height of the plants. Plant the high plants or climbers in the north end of the bed, that way they will not shade the rest of your crop from the all-important–life-giving–sunlight.

In other words, if you have a raised bed that is broadside on to the sun for most of the day, then perhaps a frame built along the back of the bed would be a good idea. This would enable you to grow runner beans, peas or cucumber plants, making an excellent backdrop to the vegetables in the rest of the bed.

Peas would have the added advantage of adding nitrogen to the soil that would ensure a great harvest from the likes of cabbage or cauliflower that are particularly nitrogen hungry plants. It is also true however, that all plants like some nitrogen in their diet of nutrients, and so this technique would benefit just about everything.

A single crop

Planting a single crop in a raised bed is usually only done if you have more than one bed in which to grow your vegetables. After all what is the point in growing just one crop, unless of course you are a fanatical pumpkin grower, or just cannot see past a good cucumber harvest!

If however you do just have one crop in mind then that is fine. Your choice however should not just be on what you like, but rather on what you have grown in the bed previously – if at all.

Good crop rotation is not only important as to the nutrient value, but also for pest control and issues such as blight and fungal growth. If you have suffered a case of potato blight the previous year for instance, then you would not want to try and grow the same crop again this year as the potato blight virus can remain in the soil for several years.

Similarly it is not a good idea to grow onions in the same bed for more than two or three years running, if you want to get the most out of your harvest.

Even with a single crop as your main crop however, you can still grow a 'companion' crop if you mix them correctly.

Companion crops are vegetables that get on well with other vegetables such as onions, carrots and lettuce or spinach onions and brassicas, being that their nutritional needs are similar, but their root systems collect the nutrients at different levels and so are not truly in direct competition with each other.

As well as giving you a variety of vegetables, this is a good idea for things such as pest control and less weeding as the veg blocks out the light to the weeds; and different crops attract different insects thereby helping control the spread of the insects themselves.

Antagonist crops are crops that do not do so well together such as Alliums (onions and garlic) with peas and bean crops. Crops such as beetroot get along with most plants and so can be planted quite successfully between onions or leeks without any problem.

Mixed crop examples

If you have just one raised bed and are trying out several varieties of vegetables to give you a good mixed crop, then some planting tips could include the following regime:
Tall plants to the back, on a fixed support of some kind where needed.

This could be planted with tomatoes, or peas, runner beans or cucumbers if the climate allows.
Sweetcorn could also be used here and companioned with lettuce that will take advantage of the shade from the corn.
To the front of the raised bed could go any low-lying crop such as carrot, beetroot, parsnips etc.

If peppers are your main crop then you could grow spinach between the pepper plants. Again similar to the lettuce and corn example, the spinach will take advantage and flourish in the shade provided by the peppers.

If you stay in a cooler climate such as the UK, then you could try covering a portion of your raised bed with a frame similar to that pictured earlier, and cover with polythene. This will enable you to grow tomatoes and cucumber plants for instance, maybe even some sweet peppers – so expensive to buy in the supermarket!

To get the most out of a mixed crop the idea is about looking at the different vegetables needs regarding hours of sunlight and nutrient requirements. A good idea is to plant vegetables together that have different root systems, as mentioned earlier.

Planting deep rooted vegetables such as carrots or parsnips, means that you can companion them with shallow rooted vegetables such as beetroot, lettuce and arugula (rocket) to make for a good health selection.

Ultimate mixed crop

We can hardly discuss the idea of a mixed crop, without including a piece on the square foot example of growing mixed vegetables.

As mentioned, this is a system that is intensive farming gone to the extreme – but in a good way! The idea is that the old method of growing vegetables in a garden plot, where everything is planted in rows, is made redundant.

Instead we have a situation where a plot of ground – raised or otherwise – is set out in squares 1 foot square. Within these mini-plots a range of vegetables are planted, according to your needs and other deciding factors such as weather, nutrients etc.

The 'sales pitch' if you like, for this style of gardening include the following points:

A large percentage of a traditional vegetable plot is wasted owing to the fact that you must have pathways between the vegetables for weeding, harvesting etc.

With a proper rotational method of planting, you need never use fertilizer again, as the crops will feed themselves.

Far less waste than a traditional garden where all the cabbages, or cauliflower or whatever, is ready at more or less the same time, and has to be frozen, canned or given away.

Similar to a raised bed, the square foot method does not need such intensive care, due to the close proximity of the plants and the ease of gardening methods, particularly if it is used with conjunction with a raised bed garden.

One of the main strengths of this gardening method is the fact that it uses up very little space, especially if you go for the four foot square method. This means that despite this small space you can grow a complete range vegetables and have them all maturing at different times, depending of course on the length of the growing season.

That said, you have to keep a keen eye on any disease or insect infestation, potentially caused by the close proximity and therefore poor air circulation, in this type of growing environment.

A square foot garden design lends itself very well to cultivating a full spectrum of herbs available. This in turn will ensure a garnish for every meal you prepare as well as some great tomato and basil salads for example.

Pest control

One of the things that mixed planting is good for is pest control, as we have mentioned the combination of different plants can confuse the pests and help control their breeding program. However there are certain plants that you do not want to mix together because they encourage the same pest. This could lead to an exacerbation of your pest problems, instead of the opposite.

For instance, if you consider pest control to be a major objective in your growing regime, it is not wise to grow sweetcorn and tomatoes together as they both attract the corn ear-worm, also known as the tomato fruit worm. Tomatoes, eggplant, peppers and potatoes are a favorite of the Colorado beetle; while squash, melons and cucumbers are a favorite snack for the pickleworm.

Pest control in a raised bed

Controlling slugs in a raised bed situation is particularly easy, compared to the traditional growing methods. Simply fix some copper tape around the edge of the raised bed; slugs will not cross copper as it has a chemical reaction to their slime. Copper paint will do as well.

There are of course the usual tips about beer traps or bran and vinegar to attract them. Either method works by setting a trap including these ingredients and hiding it under a roof tile or similar. The slugs are attracted to the traps where they can then be disposed of.
Carrot fly prevention is one of the bonuses of a raised bed as carrot fly do not tend to go over 18 inches or so, as a general rule. This means that the higher raised beds have a good advantage over the battle with carrot fly. One of the top tips to keep away the carrot fly include extending your raised bed frame

height by about one foot or so, then adding some fine insect mesh around it.

This can be very effective against the carrot fly, as they are low flyers as mentioned, and so this will prevent them from dropping by and laying their eggs on your young carrots.

In general however the advantage of the raised bed, is that it is fairly easy, especially if you have developed the cold-frame idea, to flip a fine nylon mesh over your crop. This will prevent the egg-laying butterflies and moths from getting access.

It will also prevent the birds from helping themselves either to the young seedling or indeed your strawberry harvest.

Rodents:
To keep out burrowing rodents such as moles or gophers, then you need to lay down some wire mesh on the bottom of the raised bed before you infill with the compost material. This should be a fairly sturdy galvanized mesh with about 1inch holes preferably.

This will prevent most critters from gaining access to the bed from below.
The smaller rodents such as mice or voles have to be kept away with the usual fine mesh or even fleece material, if you want to prevent them from nibbling on (or destroying completely!) your young peas and beans.

I have had some success with a battery operated sonic device for chasing mice. If you just place one of these devices anywhere in the bed, cover against the weather, and turn it on. Results have been mixed according to some of the comments I have had from others but it may well be worth a try at least if you have a bad mouse problem.

Summary

As you may have guessed by now, I am quite a fan of raised bed gardening. Yes it is true that more preparation is involved at the beginning of the project, if you are going to build a raised bed. However the rewards in my view, are well worth the effort, as the raised beds that you build should give you many years' worth of service.

Another advantage of the raised bed that I have not covered here, is simply the fact that you do not need the same range of expensive garden machinery. Rotavators for instance, usually needed to dig over the soil, are not needed for a raised bed. Most of the digging work is done with the help of a small garden fork, as the soil is generally light and loamy.

In fact almost all the tools you need are simple hand tools, for light digging and pruning of your plants.

I have been asked in the past, just what is the difference between a Raised Bed and a Planter – the answer is simple. A Raised Bed does not have a timber base, and therefore cannot be moved around. Planters do have a slatted base and are generally smaller, to enable positioning. Planters are generally chosen for ornamental purposes, though they can be used to grow vegetables very effectively..

There are areas however where there is just a fine line between one and the other – and that is fine.

FAQ'S

Q: Do I use treated or un-treated timber for this project?

A: (This has been answered to some extent in earlier chapters.) Personally I prefer to use treated timber as the whole construction will last that much longer. However I do appreciate that there may be environmental as well as possible health issues involved with using treated timber.

This concern is dealt with by lining the inside of the Raised Bed with polythene membrane, thus preventing any possible leakage from the timber into the soil. However as previously mentioned, the alternative is simple – use untreated timber. You will still get a minimum 5-7 years use out of your Bed.

Untreated Redwood or Cedar on the other hand will last for at least 10 years, but is of course more expensive.

Q: My garden is uneven, can I still do this?

A: Most certainly! Simply do as you would with any Raised Bed garden and raise one side of the bed to enable the levelling out of the growing area.

Q: Can I grow climbers such as peas and beans?

A: Yes indeed. Simply construct a timber climbing frame as you would normally and attach it to the sides of the Bed or sink posts into the ground for shallower structures.

Q: How big should my raised bed be – what dimensions?

A: Firstly there is no need to get hung-up over size, in this instance it really does not matter! However as a general guide they are usually no more than 3-4 foot wide and 6-9 foot long. This is mainly to do with access for maintenance and harvesting, as you do not really want to reach across more than 2 foot for instance.

As for height. This can be from only 4 inches (100mm) to around 2-3 foot (600-900mm) depending on your circumstances. Taller Beds mean less bending over, and easier access for wheelchair users. The downside is that they take more material to infill.

Q: Can I just infill it with soil?

A: Yes of course – but I would not recommend it, for 2 reasons. First is that soil tends to compact down in a Raised Bed. This makes it difficult to maintain. Secondly you are going to be plagued with weeds, which will be more difficult to remove in a compacted bed.

The concept behind a Raised Bed garden is that it is a 'no-dig' option for vegetable gardeners. By filling it with soil you will in effect make it a 'hard-dig' option in the long term.

Thank You!

Finally as the author, I would like to extend to you my heart-felt thanks for purchasing this book – and also for reading it!

Firstly I have to admit that despite the word 'Complete' in the title of this book, I have found that with gardening in particular there is no such thing as a 'complete' solution when it comes to growing any plants - be they vegetable, fruit or flowers.

Just like the plants themselves, techniques or systems for growing evolve pretty much to suit our lifestyles or indeed budgets. However the basics remain the same.

Sunlight, nutrients, water, warmth. Put them together in the right measure, add a little care, and you will grow excellent plants – no green fingers involved!

I hope you have enjoyed this short book on Raised Bed gardening – and maybe picked up a tip or two that will be of benefit to you in your gardening efforts.

James Paris

MY NOTES / TO-DO PAGE

MY NOTES / TO-DO PAGE

MY NOTES / TO-DO PAGE

16236120R00041

Printed in Great Britain
by Amazon